How Are Rocks Formed?

If...Then

Amanda Vink

COMPUTER SCIENCE For the REAL World™

Rosen Classroom™

Published in 2018 by The Rosen Publishing Group, Inc.
29 East 21st Street, New York, NY 10010

Book Design: Jennifer Ryder-Talbot
Editor: Caitie McAneney

Photo Credits: Cover, photogal/Shutterstock.com; pp. 4-5 Frank Chen/Shutterstock.com; p. 6 Martin Gillman/Shutterstock.com; p. 9 Willyam Bradberry/Shutterstock.com; pp. 10-11 Ozgur Coskun/Shutterstock.com; p. 12 Redchanka/Shutterstock.com; p. 15 keiki/Shutterstock.com; p. 16 Albert Russ/Shutterstock.com; p. 17 Peter Hermes Furian/Shutterstock.com; p. 18-19 turtix/Shutterstock.com; p. 20 Danie Nel Photography/Shutterstock.com; p. 21 bubblea/Shutterstock.com.

Library of Congress Cataloging-in-Publication Data

Names: Vink, Amanda.
Title: How are rocks formed?: if...then / Amanda Vink.
Description: New York : Rosen Classroom, 2018. | Series: Computer Kids: Powered by Computational Thinking | Includes glossary and index.
Identifiers: LCCN ISBN 9781538353028 (pbk.) | ISBN 9781538324004 (library bound) | ISBN 9781538353288 (6 pack) | ISBN 9781508137221 (ebook)
Subjects: LCSH: Rocks--Juvenile literature. | Geology--Juvenile literature.
Classification: LCC QE432.2 V56 2018 | DDC 552--dc23

Manufactured in the United States of America

CPSIA Compliance Information: Batch #WS18RC: For Further Information contact Rosen Publishing, New York, New York at 1-800-237-9932

Table of Contents

The Rock Cycle

Have you ever collected rocks? If so, you might have noticed that many rocks look the same and many look different. The three different kinds of rock on Earth are igneous, sedimentary, and metamorphic. They look different because they are created differently. All three kinds of rock are part of the rock **cycle**.

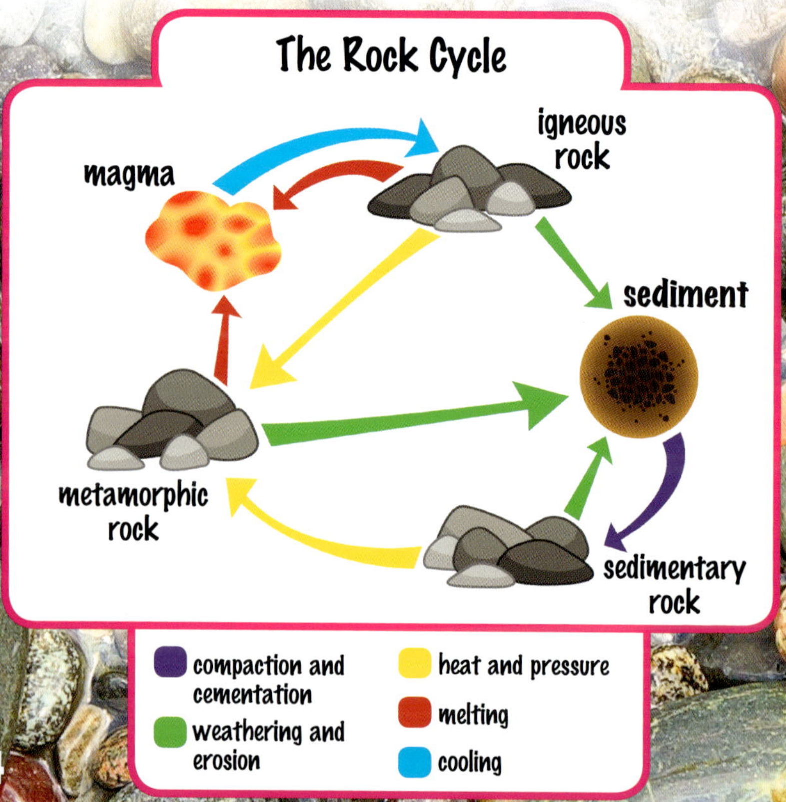

The rock cycle is a series of changes a rock can go through. If igneous rock is broken down, then it can become small pieces called sediment. If sediment is **compacted**, then they can be made into sedimentary rock. Learning how the rock cycle works can tell you a lot about how rocks are made, where they are found, and what they look like.

The diagram on the left shows the rock cycle.

Rocks are made of one or more minerals. You might be familiar with a diamond, which is a mineral.

What Are Rocks Made Of?

If you look around, then you'll notice that rocks are found just about everywhere! Rocks make up the non-water part of the outermost layer of the earth, which is called the crust.

All rocks are made of one or more minerals. Minerals are naturally occurring solid **substances** that have the same fixed structure. If you have ever looked at a diamond or an emerald, then you've seen a mineral! Other minerals you may be familiar with are quartz and graphite. Rocks may also contain organic **compounds** that are associated with living things. A rock generally doesn't have a uniform structure, so scientists describe a rock by how it was made or by where it fits in the rock cycle.

Melting and Cooling

The Latin word *ignis* means "fire," which perfectly describes an igneous rock! These rocks come from magma, or molten rock, that **originates** deep within the earth. At that depth, temperatures are **extremely** hot. But as the magma moves upward toward the crust, it cools and hardens when temperatures become less extreme. If the molten rock hardens below the surface, then it is called intrusive rock. These rocks cool very slowly, which results in large crystals.

If magma erupts from a volcano, then it is called lava. When the lava hardens into rock, it is called extrusive rock. Extrusive rocks harden very quickly because they are exposed to the cooler temperatures of the air. The crystals in extrusive rocks are very small.

Igneous rocks are formed from magma or lava.

Monumental Igneous Rocks

There are more than 700 different types of igneous rock. The size of the crystals in both intrusive and extrusive igneous rocks can help you tell them apart. Some extrusive rocks have crystals so small you can't see them without a microscope!

Granite is a kind of intrusive igneous rock that is very useful for humans. It is often used in construction

Mount Rushmore in South Dakota was carved into granite.

because it is very hard. A famous **monument** made of granite is Mount Rushmore, which honors four American presidents. The monument was carved into a granite peak in South Dakota.

Obsidian is a type of extrusive igneous rock. It is volcanic glass, and it can be cut to be extremely sharp. Obsidian was used by early civilizations to make arrowheads, spear points, and knife blades.

Fossils are the imprints of animals and plants that lived long ago.

Layers of Rocks

Over time, wind and rain break down existing rocks on Earth's surface. This process is called **erosion**. If water picks up sediment as it flows downstream, then the sediment is carried to other places. If sediment starts to build up layer by layer, then it becomes extremely heavy. The weight cements everything into a solid rock, called sedimentary rock.

Sedimentary rocks make up only about five percent of the types of rocks found in the earth's crust. However, they make up the majority of rocks found at the surface where humans live. Most fossils can be found in sedimentary rock. Fossils are the impression, or imprint, of the remains of animals and plants that lived on Earth thousands to billions of years ago. Do you have any fossils?

Sedimentary Rocks

You may be using sedimentary rock right in your home! Shale forms from layers of silt, sand, and mud. It is remarkable because it is fissile, or can be split easily. Some shale can be broken down into little bits, mixed with water, and used to make clay. This clay is used to make bricks, roof tiles, and flowerpots.

Chalk is made from limestone, which is sedimentary rock made mostly of calcium carbonate from deposits of shells and coral in deep water. This type of chalk was used to write on chalkboards before it was made from a more common mineral called gypsum. If you want to see an impressive structure made from chalk, then visit the White Cliffs of Dover in Kent, England.

The White Cliffs of Dover in Kent, England, are a great example of sedimentary rock.

Juan de Fuca Plate
North American Plate
Cocos Plate
Caribbean Plate
Pacific Plate
Nazca Plate
South American Plate
Scotia Plate
Eurasian Plate
Arabian Plate
African Plate
Indian Plate
Phillipine Sea Plate
Pacific Plate
Australian Plate
Antarctic Plate

Metamorphic Rocks

If an existing igneous or sedimentary rock is altered, or changed, by physical or chemical forces, then it becomes a metamorphic rock. Any rock can become a metamorphic rock. The earth's crust is made of multiple tectonic plates, or large areas of rock that shift around. Tectonic plates smash into one another over time. These movements create mountains and bodies of water, such as lakes or oceans.

The high heat and pressure involved with this movement warps and changes preexisting rocks. These rocks change shape and can get very dense and heavy. They can end up looking very different! Metamorphic rocks can melt to become igneous rocks again, or they can come to the surface to break down and eventually form sedimentary rocks.

Large tectonic plates make up the earth's crust.

After Transformation

Marble is an example of a metamorphic rock. Originally, marble is the sedimentary rock limestone, but during metamorphic **transformation** the crystals change and become larger. The fossils from sea plants and animals in the limestone can no longer be seen once they are subjected to high heat and pressure.

Marble is a beautiful stone, and it is used to make many monuments. The Taj Mahal, one of the New Seven Wonders of the World, is an immense **mausoleum** built in Agra, India. The outside of the Taj Mahal is made of white marble.

Slate is a metamorphic rock that was originally shale. Slate has been used throughout the world to make roofing and floors, since it can be cut into thin sheets and keeps water out.

The impressive Taj Mahal in India has a facade, or outside layer, made of white marble.

The rock cycle never stops!

Rocks Change!

A rock is constantly changing due to erosion, heat, or physical pressure. Still, it takes a very long time for it to go through the rock cycle. It takes thousands of years for a rock to go through the process! All rocks take a different journey through the rock cycle. If a rock starts as a sedimentary rock and changes to a metamorphic rock, then it may break down into sediments and become a sedimentary rock again. It could also melt and become an igneous rock.

The cycle keeps going, and rocks never stay exactly as they are right now. Take a close look at your rock collection. In a few thousand years those rocks may look very different!

Rocks Are Important

Rocks are an important part of our society. Humans have used rocks as the tools for building civilizations. We use rocks to make the buildings we live in. We use rocks to make tools for farming and making food products, which brings food to our stores and to our tables. We use rocks to make the jewelry we wear. The igneous rock obsidian is even used in medical surgery since it can be made sharper than steel!

The rock cycle shows how the earth is constantly changing through the **formation**, breakdown, and reformation of minerals and organic materials. The rock cycle has shaped the planet for billions of years, and it will continue to do so. If you hold a rock, then you hold a piece of history!

Glossary

compact: To force closer together.

compound: Something formed by combining two parts.

cycle: A series of things that repeats.

erosion: The act of wearing away by water, wind, or ice.

extreme: Great or severe.

formation: The act of forming or creating something.

mausoleum: A large tomb.

monument: A lasting evidence, reminder, or example of someone or something notable or great.

originate: Start.

sediment: Matter, such as stones and sand, that is carried onto land or into the water by wind, water, or land movement.

substance: Matter of a certain chemical makeup.

transformation: The act of changing or being changed.

Index